# How to Revise the Quick and Easy Way

*A Realistic and Effective Guide to Stress Free Revision, to Optimise Performance in any Exam Scenario*

*Alan Starr*

How to Revise the Quick and Easy Way
Published by Little Green Lizard Publications
Cold Mill Road
UK

First Edition Published 2021
Printed in Great Britain
ISBN: 9798771406381

# Disclaimer

**Disclaimer notice**
Please note the information contained within this document is for educational and entertainment purposes only. All effort has been executed to present accurate up-to-date and reliable complete information. No warranties of any kind are declared or implied. Readers acknowledge that the author is not engaging in the rendering of legal, financial, medical or professional advice. The content within this book has been derived from various sources.

Under no circumstances will any blame or legal responsibility be held against the publisher or author for any damages, reparation or monetary loss due to information contained within this book either directly or indirectly.

By reading this document, the reader agrees that under no circumstances is the author responsible for any losses, direct or indirect which are incurred as a result of the use of the information contained within this document, including but not limited to, errors, omissions or inaccuracies.

# Table of Contents

# Introduction

Your exams are around the corner and you should be preparing. Everyone around you seems to be revising and everyone you talk to seems to have their head in a book, except you. Have you left it too late? Perhaps you think you have a lot of time? The truth is, if you can see other people revising, then the chances are you should be too. You know you should be revising, you know what revising is, but you're not too sure exactly how to do it effectively. Are you even doing it correctly? Everyone you speak to has a different technique or method. Some people might say that all they do is read, but that just seems too time-consuming and work heavy, and let's be honest, you have a social life to maintain.

As time is progressing, exams are getting closer and you know you need to start revising and need to take a positive step in the right direction. After all, if you don't take a positive step in the right direction, panic mode starts, then worry sets in and you will not be sitting exams in the right frame of mind. Your performance will be poor and last minute and the years of preparation will have been for nothing.

This book will demonstrate to you that, you can revise using a very simple, effective and easy to apply method consistently. You will learn how to create the correct environment and work ethic as well as apply the most effective revision techniques, producing revision notes that are detailed and concise and promoting optimal performance. This is based on seventeen years of teaching experience at all levels, helping students successfully revise for exams and progress onto apprenticeships, A-Levels and university courses.

Achieving success is your goal and this book will help improve your ability to take effective revision notes, in an easy way to optimise your exam performance and achieve the best possible outcome for you. The techniques and methods will seem so obvious, you'll be wondering why you hadn't been doing this previously. The truth is that often some people overlook the easy solutions, believing that the more complex ones are the most effective, whereas usually it's quite the opposite.

If you read this book to the end, you will be a more effective learner, achieve much higher grades, increase your potential as a student and prove any doubters wrong, but, more importantly, you will have a technique that you can apply whenever you want, to retain information and make revision so much easier in the future.

In addition to this, you will also learn the fundamentals relevant to becoming mentally and physically prepared to analyse and absorb information rich sources and retain key knowledge easily. You will learn the importance of establishing a solid learning environment and exactly what apparatus you will need to optimise performance and create a positive mind-set for your exams. So, what are you waiting for? You are an hour read away from becoming a learning machine. You are within reach of your goal and you too, can look like you're revising hard and can be more prepared than most, for your upcoming exams. So, let's get started!

# Chapter 1: How to Unlock Your True Learning Potential

In this section we will be discussing what revision is and what you can do to revise more efficiently. We will be exploring the different learning styles and what they mean and also recognise the most ineffective and inefficient techniques, which the vast majority of people tend to pursue. We will also discuss how you can avoid falling into the revision 'trap' that so many are inclined to do, wasting valuable time and energy on inefficient revision techniques, as they just go through the motions.

I think before we start, it's important to address why schools and universities don't teach revision. The answer is actually quite simple, it is not on the national curriculum. The national curriculum is what the teachers have to teach; it is the content of the courses. There is simply no time to teach the plethora of different revision techniques to meet the individual needs of a range of students. Each student learns in different ways and to try and accommodate all of these will effectively take time away from the curriculum, meaning that the content won't be covered and you will not be appropriately prepared with the correct information, to successfully complete your exams. Therefore, the responsibility falls on your shoulders, to take the time to revise the content. It's harsh but true, but don't worry, because you will now be equipped with the essential tools and skills required to maximise your performance and achieve your full potential.

So, let's start with the basics: what is revision? Revision, in the context of preparing for an exam, is re-familiarising yourself with information that you already know. You cannot revise information that you do not already know, therefore if you are unfamiliar with a topic, may I recommend that you seek out the subject teacher for support and guidance.

Revision can come in many forms, depending on your learning style and work ethic. The different types of learning styles include:

**Auditory**: This category of learner is someone who learns through listening. Often an auditory learner will need to have instructions and information presented in audio form, as they find it difficult to interpret written information such as instructions or directions. Auditory learners are good at listening and reciting information. Some people find it difficult to learn through just listening and lose concentration during the lesson. If you find that during the lesson you tend to doodle, it could be that you are not best suited to this form of learning, but instead are a visual learner.

**Visual:** A visual learner is someone who studies using images or videos to organise and arrange ideas. Visual learners enjoy learning from diagrams and often doodle or draw images such as diagrams to help communicate a message. I am a visual learner and find it easier to draw and doodle notes, in a story form, as it is easier to read. This style of learning is not for everybody, but if it works for me that's all that matters as everyone's learning needs differ.

**Kinaesthetic:** A kinaesthetic learner is someone who learns through practical activity such as model making or conducting an experiment. Kinaesthetic learners are able to recite ideas and information having undertook the task in a practical fashion. This 'learning through doing' approach is really helpful because you are able to experience the mistakes first-hand and are able to recall information based on your experience and not on what somebody's told you. However, when revising to a strict timescale, it can be impractical.

**Reading and Writing:** Someone who learns effectively through reading information and writing it down tends to make extensive notes, which can look impressive, but it's not always practical especially if it's not your natural learning style. This is the most common form of revision, but not the most efficient. Although revision can include writing, it is difficult to know exactly how much to write. When do you stop? What do you write? What's important? What do you need to know?

If my years of experience have taught me anything, it is that most of these techniques can be incorporated into one very simple method and can be applied regardless of your specific learning style. The glory of teaching is that techniques and methods evolve and our job as teachers is to be adaptable and modify the things that work effectively.

So, which learning style best suits you? I am sure you can identify with one of the learning styles, which means that you have already unlocked a huge part of the learning and revision process; knowing how you learn most effectively is going to give you the key and the power to access and retain information and help you achieve your full potential in any exam scenario. In theory, just knowing this alone will be a wake-up call and make you realise how obvious and straightforward this is. However, often people will believe that if they are not reading and writing information and doing exactly what they see others doing, then they are not learning effectively, which is not the case.

The reading and writing learning style is probably the most dangerous of all the learning styles. It will work for some people, but what tends to happen is that if you don't know what good information looks like, you will often simply copy out all of the original notes, believing that this is the correct thing to do. Ultimately, what you are left with is a complete duplicate of your original notes! Is that revision? I promise, you will be spending more time making sure your work is neat and spelt correctly, rather than identifying key facts and components that are essential to the revision process. This means that you now have double the amount of work and have wasted a lot of time, effort and energy and are back at square one. Whereas if you work smart, you could have less than a quarter of the notes but all of the key information, and the best part is, you will also have more downtime to spend with your family or friends, which is essential to the revision process. Which would you prefer?

In summary, good revision techniques and methods must fit into your own learning style and natural way of work. You cannot shoehorn someone else's technique, into your way of work as it will feel awkward, un-natural and will not be productive. You will in effect just be going through the motions, hoping that something will happen, when in fact, all you are generating is waste paper. That's the reality. So, let's discuss the process of turning you into a learning machine. Don't worry, I promise that it is so easy, you'll wish you'd been doing this years ago.

# Chapter: 2: Simple Foods to Improve Brain Function

The Internet is littered with methods, techniques and gimmicks that people believe to be the best when it comes to revising or retaining information. The problem is, of the millions of techniques and methods available, which do you use? Coming from a teaching perspective, I understand, that often, I am dealing with a generation of learners who naturally want the "quick fix", "easy solution" or "hack". This only makes sense; after all, why would you want to waste time trawling through revision notes, writing down information that you don't even know is relevant, but blindly copy down, just in case? Therefore, with this experience I can tell you that effective revision is more than just finding the right technique. Imagine you're going on a car journey. Ask yourself what makes this journey comfortable? I mean really think about it. Is it the comfortable seats? Is it the smooth wheels gliding against the even road surface? Is it the fact that you can listen to music? Is it because the engine is running smooth and quiet? I think you'll find the answer is all of the above. You will not have a comfortable journey if you have flat tyres but comfortable seating. Equally, you will not have a comfortable journey if your seats are comfortable your tyres are inflated, but you've used the wrong oil in the engine or low-grade fuel in the tank. The point I'm trying to make is that, for you to be an effective revision machine, there are several factors to make the process run smooth and optimise how you perform.

These are the physical attributes that will make your journey comfortable, therefore, it stands to reason that before we explore any revision techniques or methods, we must first look at what physical preparation you can undertake, to make sure your revision journey runs effectively, efficiently and with ease.

### Physical Preparation

There are a whole range of things that you can do to physically prepare for the demands of exam preparation. However, I've isolated it down to five key areas that I believe to be the most important and have stripped the information down to be easily digested and simple to apply. I promise not to go all 'sciencey' and appreciate time is of the essence so let's move forward.

### Sleep

Often, I hear stories about how students revise hard into the night often getting no sleep and operating on a diet of caffeine, to try and get a few extra 'valuable' minutes revision time. The problem is that the body requires sleep as part of your revision process. Unfortunately, this does not mean that you can sleep your way to University, but you can take advantage of the psychological benefits that sleep provides. It is regularly stated that sleep helps organise information learned that day and also helps replenish the brain to become fresh and ready to absorb more information. Therefore, it stands to reason that if you do not get the recommended amount of sleep, it is likely to result in poor performance in an exam scenario. Remember the car example? A comfortable journey is not just in the seats and upholstery of the car: if the tyres are flat the car will not move effectively, resulting in a bumpy ride.

**Water**

Water is the fuel for the machine. Although it provides no energy, the benefits are vast, after all we are made up of 70% water. Water hydrates the brain, the body and the skin and helps to flush out toxins. Toxins can make the body operate ineffectively, which inevitably means performance will suffer. It is the reason why your teacher allows you to have a water bottle on your desk and not a can of energy drink. The energy drink does not provide the same benefits as water and can have a negative effect on how you perform in school, due to the additives, sugars and sometimes high caffeine content. Dehydration can cause headaches, poor focus, and migraines and can make your going to toilet a lot less regular, which means you'll get a toxic build-up making you feel awful. It seems easy and straightforward but is often neglected. The best part is that it's an easy addition to your regime and is readily at hand. To refer back to the car example if the car is running on low-grade oil or low-grade fuel it is not likely to work quite as efficiently in the long run.

**Exercise**

Exercise isn't always about getting 'gains' or being 'shredded'. Exercise is anything that increases your heart rate. If you are increasing your heart rate you are pumping oxygen to the parts the body that need it the most. A simple half hour walk in the morning will provide you with fresh air making you feel more awake and alert and ready to begin work. Sat indoors for prolonged periods of time can result in poor movement, inactivity, stiff joints, aches and pains which will all have an impact on how you perform in an exam scenario. They say a fit body is a fit mind and that makes sense. If you refer to the car example, if a car was to stay in the garage and remain inactive, parts of the car would begin to seize up. The oil and fuel tanks would begin to clog and the car would not run smoothly if at all. You do not need a gym membership to do exercise; it is recommended that 10,000 steps provides adequate exercise and is easy to do with minimal equipment required.

Exercise also releases endorphins which make you feel happy and positive and help to suppress negative feelings. Exercise such as running swimming or HIIT (high-intensity interval training) all have a positive effect on fitness and well-being, which will improve your attitude and work productivity as you will be approaching your work with a more positive mind-set. Information is more likely to be retained, as you will be less distracted as you're not feeling bored, irritated or negative. You will work harder with more focus over a sustained period of time.

## Diet

Diet is hugely important in the lead up to exams, as what you put into your body is going to be processed and used to help your body function. Just because we've used the word diet, does not mean we have to lose weight to do revision, nor does it mean we need to bulk up. Instead, it means we have to compliment what we already eat with the right kind of nutrients, to ensure our bodies have a fighting chance of working as effectively as possible. The more nutrient dense foods you can incorporate into your everyday diet, the better you will feel and you'll be able to concentrate on revision with more focus and energy. Junk food is likely to make your body work in a more sluggish and unproductive fashion, whereas fresh, nutrient rich foods, are much more likely to provide your body with the necessary vitamins and nutrients required for your body to work at an optimal level. I know it seems obvious, but it is often something people overlook for a more convenient fast alternative. Healthy foods do not have to be inconvenient and come in many easy to eat, 'grab and go' forms. Below is a list of five important nutrients that will have a positive impact on how your body performs in the lead up to exams and during revision.

**Top Brain Foods**

**Flavonoids**
Flavonoids are believed to promote better memory and will help support optimal performance in a revision scenario. One excellent source of flavonoids is dark chocolate which is readily available and relatively affordable, in any

supermarket. Dark chocolate needs to be high in cocoa content to get the full nutritional benefit. Chocolate also tastes amazing and will lift your mood and make you feel good and more positive. Citrus fruits are also believed to contain flavonoids and are also easy to access and very affordable. This is a basic list of easy to access 'grab and go' foods that will promote optimal performance:

**Vitamin C**

Vitamin C is found in many fruits and is responsible for supporting a healthy immune system. Citrus fruit such as oranges or grapefruit are also very watery, which helps hydrate your body and detoxify. Additionally, citrus fruits are also believed to contain flavonoids which lift the mood and improve memory. Another benefit of citrus fruits includes high fibre content which helps support a healthy digestive system and prevent a toxic backlog, which would otherwise cause headaches, migraines and a poor sense of wellbeing. Citrus fruit is readily accessible and quite affordable and is an excellent easy addition to any everyday diet. It is recommended that you have five fruit and veg a day, to feed your body with the adequate nutrition required.

## Vitamin B6

Vitamin B6 is an essential vitamin for energy and can be found in nuts and bananas as well as other foods. These nutrient rich foods are very affordable and can be consumed on the go. The good thing about nuts and bananas is that they keep for a long time, so you can dip in and out and don't have the pressure of eating by the sell by date.

Nuts are filled with good fats, fats that your body needs to function. It is believed that your brain is 60% fat, therefore it makes perfect sense that if you want your brain to function properly, you need to feed it with the correct nutrition. Nuts are also an excellent source of fibre which will help regulate your digestive system and expel toxins. On a side note, this source of B6 is also good for hair and nails so you will look amazing when revising. Try to consume nuts that have not been salted, because salted nuts will cause dehydration and excess salt has negative health implications. Nuts such as unsalted walnuts and almonds are excellent.

Bananas are an excellent source of potassium as well as vitamin B6. In addition to this, they are also a good source of fibre and contain powerful antioxidants that will help your body expel toxins resulting in a more effective engine. This fruit also contains potassium which supports muscle health and the nervous system, therefore, it could be said that potassium is very beneficial in supporting brain function. Bananas are convenient and cost-effective way of getting many health benefits on the go. They can also help you regulate blood sugar and provide you with a more sustained energy source throughout the day.

## Vitamin B12

B12 is another vitamin that is known to support brain health, as well as having other benefits. This is commonly found in cereals, milk and eggs, which are all very easy additions to any start to the day and are packed full of a range of nutrients not just B12. Milk is commonly known for its calcium content but also contains B12, among other nutrients, while eggs are filled with protein and other vitamins and nutrients as well as good fats that are essential in providing the body with the necessary tools to build and be strong.

Cereal is one of the easiest ways to get a range of vitamins and nutrients in the morning. You can read the side of any cereal box and see the full range of health benefits it provides. However, you need to make sure that you check the sugar content, because some cereals, although providing a range of vitamins and nutrients, can also include large amounts of sugar. Sugar will make the cereals sweeter and more desirable, but sugar will peak your energy levels which will then plummet, making you feel low, irritable, hungry and sluggish. Energy sources, such as low sugar cereals, as well as fruits such as bananas, provide you with a more sustained energy source, which means there are no high peaks and no extreme lows: your energy will remain consistent throughout the day, you will feel energised, fresh and will be able to concentrate more effectively on the task without the negatives.

**Vitamin D3**

D3 is probably one of the hardest vitamins to acquire during any day, never the less, it can also be one of the easiest. Vitamin D3 comes from the sun and apparently you only need to be in the sun for twenty minutes to get the full benefits. However, it is also one of the hardest to acquire because if you live in a country that is often not sunny, sources of Vitamin D3 become difficult and expensive to acquire.

Vitamin D3 can also be found in oily fish, but if you are not a big fan of oily fish (and I know my target audience), there are supplements that you can take to ensure that you get your recommended daily allowance. Ideally, you want to consume vitamins in the most natural form, however, vitamin D3 could be an exception, due to how difficult it is to acquire. Vitamin D also promotes healthy brain function and it is also good for the immune system.

**Vitamin E**

Vitamin E is essential for brain development because it helps to expel oxygen free radicals and has antioxidant properties. This vital vitamin can be found in nuts as well as other foods but nuts are easily accessible and there are a large variety readily available. Nuts are so popular and so beneficial, they now come in a range of spreads, butters and milk. If you don't like nuts you can still get the great nutritional benefits by drinking almond milk or hazelnut milk and provide your body with the valuable nutrients it needs to function at an optimal level. They are essential because they are filled with good fats that your body needs and are also very fibrous which means that they can promote good digestive health and expel toxins, which will make you feel better and less sluggish.

Vegetables are also a good source of Vitamin E among other vitamins. Cruciferous or green leafy vegetables such as spinach or kale are particularly excellent and nutrient dense. Although very beneficial to your body, it is not always easy to pick up a bag of kale or spinach and eat it on the go, whereas nuts make an ideal snack that is much more convenient. That's not to say you should neglect all vegetables in favour of nuts but if we're thinking quick, cost-effective and easy, then that's the way to go.

**Omega 3**
Without going too "sciencey" omega-3 is very beneficial to brain health and your performance. This essential nutrient is largely found in fish and among other foods but these are the easiest to access. It is not uncommon to see Omega-3 added to other products such as spreads, which makes it easier to access and consume.

In summary, the best foods you can consume for optimal brain health often include good fats, high fibre, vitamins and nutrients, which are all the makings of a good diet. However, the foods outlined in the previous section include nutrients specific to brain health and cognitive support. The key is that if you can consume these foods in an easy "grab and go" format, then they should be easy to incorporate into your diet. However, if it is more convenient to consume vitamin tablets, as opposed to source the vitamins and nutrients naturally, then that is at least better than nothing. The only problem is that you won't reap the other health benefits that the foods provide.

## Top Foods to Avoid

This section is likely to be much shorter than the previous section because there has been a lot of press and literature to support the information below. You don't need to be an expert to know that consuming excessive amounts of sugar, caffeine and drinking alcohol is not a good idea to maximise your performance, in any situation. Below is a list of the top five foods to avoid in the lead up to exams:

## Caffeine

Caffeine is a definite no-go area when it comes to preparing for exams and trying to maintain concentration. Caffeine is a stimulant and is likely to make you irritable and affect your sleep pattern. It has already been explained that sleep can play an important part of the revision process as it prepares your brain by organising your thoughts and making you feel replenished ready for new information. Therefore, if caffeine affects your sleep pattern your brain will not get the required rest which will mean that you will feel tired, sluggish, ill-prepared, irritable and demotivated. Therefore, to achieve optimal performance, avoid caffeine during exam preparation and throughout your exams to maintain optimal performance.

## Sugar

Sugar is everywhere but is largely prevalent in soft drinks and sweets. It is also hidden in other foods such as ready meals, food dressings, juice, bread and even crisps, and so is very easy to over consume. The issue is that sugar spikes your energy levels, initially making you feel full of energy. However, this spike in energy quickly plummets making you feel sluggish and irritable. You will not be able to perform at your optimal level in any revision or exam scenario. The best thing to do is consume complex carbohydrates that provide you with a more sustained energy source throughout the day. This will avoid peaks in energy and huge dips and will also help prevent sugar cravings and hunger pangs. It is also healthier to monitor your sugar intake for general health. Food such as oats, potato, pasta or bananas are an excellent source of complex carbs. All are easily accessible and very affordable.

## Alcohol

It made the list for obvious reasons, but consuming alcohol is not a good idea during any stage of your revision. You should not be consuming alcohol anyway! The widely publicised effects of alcohol clearly demonstrate that your focus will be affected, your memory and coordination will be hindered, you'll be very dehydrated, and you will feel awful. You will definitely not perform at your optimum level consuming alcohol and need to think more carefully about your goals and whether you are taking them seriously.

**Saturated Fats**

Saturated fats are notoriously bad for you. They are linked to and associated with a whole range of health problems from obesity to non-alcoholic liver disease, clogged arteries and high blood pressure. So, it makes perfect sense that if you want to perform at the highest level you need to stay clear of those foods that are likely to prevent your body from performing and increasing the risk of health problems. In the short-term saturated fats can increase weight and make you feel sluggish and tired and give you brain fog. Therefore, it is fair to say that high saturated fatty foods are definitely a no-go area. Takeaway foods fall into this category as they are very high in fat content, but also very high in sugar and sometimes MSG an additive to flavour foods. No athlete has ever said that their training regime involves several takeaway meals and there is a reason why.

In summary, diet and food is an important part of how you perform in preparation for exams. Nutrient dense foods that are high in fibre, prepare your body ready for the journey ahead. It would be fantastic to think that all you needed to do to improve revision was to eat the correct foods, however, it's not quite as simple as that. If we refer back to the car example, a car that has top grade fuel and top-grade oil remains stationary, if there is nobody in the driving seat providing control and direction. You have provided your engine with the correct fuel; we now need to control the engine, to get to your destination. So, to move on, we will now be looking at some very simple things that you can do mentally, to prepare you for revision and exams and increase your chances of performing at the optimal level.

# Chapter 3: Getting the Edge Over Your Revision

Developing the edge and psychological advantage in an exam situation is important. Preparing for an exam is no different to a professional boxer preparing for a fight; careful consideration needs to be placed on the boxer's diet as well as mental preparation in advance of the bout. Often if the boxer has the mental advantage over his opponent, it gives the boxer the upper hand. This is best demonstrated in pre-match conferences, where boxers will face off and try to out psych their opponent, but how can you apply this technique to revision and any exam scenario?

Obviously, this does not mean that you can out psyche the exam, but it does mean, that if you are mentally and physically prepared, you will be able to face the exam ready and without fear or nerves, which will make you feel relaxed and confident, helping you to perform at the optimal level. Below, you'll see several examples of how you can gain the psychological advantage, in preparation for your exams. This will also help you to deal with pressure and help organise your thoughts, so that you feel more relaxed and more able to process information confidently and easily.

## Revision Timetable

To have an effective revision strategy you must first develop a solid and realistic revision timetable. To simply say you're going to give up four hours revision time for one subject, the day before an exam, is not only impractical but also not realistic or achievable. Four hours is far too long to spend revising and can actually be counterproductive if completed the day before the actual exam. There will be a sense of urgency and panic which will result in poor focus and poor concentration and an information overload which will cause mental fatigue and poor sleep. The most effective thing to do is develop a revision timetable. This plan for what you intend to do must include opportunities within the day, that you can spend dedicated to the revision of different subjects.

Everyone has a different type of revision timetable but as long as you have some sort of realistic achievable plan that works for you, that is all that really matters. If you work on a weekly basis and evenly distribute your subjects across the week you should cover all of your areas of focus with a shared distribution of time; aim to allocate one solid hour of quality revision time per subject, per day as a rule of thumb. Revision isn't a onetime thing and there is no overnight solution, however there are easy things that you can do to make the process run much smoother and become less of a chore. You can download revision timetables online with basic outlines as to what you should do: they are all usually free.  Most are very similar and there is no timetable that is better than another. The most important thing is that you stick to it, otherwise a revision backlog will build up and you will become overwhelmed. Make sure you revise at appropriate times and stick to the plan!

**Have a Break!**

Revision isn't all about trying to get as much information crammed in as possible. Believe it or not, revision is also about giving the brain opportunities to relax and process information. Therefore, it is important, to ensure that your revision timetable, has plenty of opportunities to have a break. Time away from your studies will then give you the opportunity to reflect on what you have done, get some fresh air, maybe enjoy a little snack and give your brain the chance to process information. You will feel less overwhelmed this way and not quite as fatigued as somebody who tries to cram three solid hours of revision in the day before an exam. You will always feel fresh, ready and prepared.

Below you will see some top suggestions that you can do during your break to ensure that you feel fresh, ready and prepared and give you the psychological edge over your revision. You will also see some things that it would be best to avoid to ensure you are always at your best.

**Top Five Things to do at Break Time**

A planned break is a good opportunity for you to give yourself something to look forward to during the revision process, but also provides your brain with a chance to digest some of the information that it has been presented with. However, the term 'break' means different things to different people. To spend one hour revising English Literature and then have a break which involves you turning the music up loud and playing on the computer, is not going to give your brain a chance to process the information because it is being overstimulated and distracted. Instead, you want your break to include quiet opportunities that will provide your brain with a respite from revision but the opportunity to process the information it has just been fed.

### 1. Go for a Walk

Going for a walk is a simple but effective way to provide your brain with the peace and quiet it needs, to process information without being overly stimulated. Going for a walk also provides your brain with exercise and oxygen required to function at an optimal level. Still, stagnant air can cause you to become sluggish and tired, whereas going for a walk is stimulating and refreshing. Also, going for a walk provides the opportunity to get Vitamin D from the sun, which is excellent for brain health and the immune system.

### 2.  Have a Light Snack

Incorporating a light snack into your revision plan during break time, is a good way to provide your brain with nutrients to stay fresh and ready and avoid mental fatigue. It is also a quiet way to break the revision process and give yourself the opportunity to sit down to reflect on your progress so far. Nutrient dense foods, as mentioned previously, are all great additions to any break.

### 3.  Talk to Someone (positive)

Taking some time out to talk to somebody, albeit a family member or friend, is also a good way to spend your break time between revision sessions. You can discuss your progress so far and how you feel you've performed or you can discuss upcoming plans. The choice of discussion is yours but try to keep it positive because a positive mind-set leads to positive performance. You don't want to call your friend and listen to how their revision isn't going very well, or hasn't even started, or that they are going out, because that will get you down and cloud your thought process. Negativity is contagious and will slowly bleed into your life if you let it.

### 4. Sit and Reflect on Your Progress

Sometimes it's nice just to sit and reflect on your progress. How's the revision going so far? As expected? If not, why? How can you make it better next time? Reflecting on your progress will mean that you have more control over how you perform and how effective your performance in an exam is likely to be. You know you're learning style and you know what you enjoy doing most, so don't be afraid to make some small changes if it means performance is likely to improve.

### 5. Review or Modify Plans

Sometimes the revision is going so well that you develop confidence and feel more prepared in some subjects more than others. This could be for several reasons. It could be that you are also revising in school with the subject teacher and feel refreshed with the subject content, or it could mean that your revision process is working really well and you feel more confident in your knowledge, based on the revision that you have done and the time you've put in. It makes sense that if you are more confident in some subjects more than others, you may want to modify the revision timetable to include more opportunities to revise those subjects that you feel least confident in. Don't be afraid to make these modifications, because you can always revert back to the original plan if it doesn't work out.

**Top Five Things to Avoid During a Break**

Although it is tempting to listen to music during your break, it will not provide your brain with adequate time to digest and process information that it has just been presented with. Listening to music, particularly loud music, will cause distraction and overstimulation which will create a poor environment for learning and retaining information. The break is not just for you but for your brain as well, so think carefully about your choices because it could affect or undo your hard efforts. Have you ever tried to listen to what someone is saying whilst typing? It's the same principle, something's got to give and you don't want your quality revision time to fall victim.

### 1. Playing Games

Playing computer games either on your phone or games consoles, is something you should try to avoid during your break. Games can be addictive and can drag out which means that if you get drawn into the game it could run into your revision time. Also, playing games can lead to a negative mind-set which will put you in the wrong frame of mind for your revision or other exam prep. Games are also overstimulating and can affect your brain's ability to process information and replenish. Doing things such as listening to loud music and playing computer games will bombard your brain with information. Give your brain a fighting chance and treat it with respect and it will pay you back.

### 2. Calling Friends for a Chat

Although it might seem like a natural thing to do during a break, calling or texting friends for a chat is not recommended. Sometimes conversations go on longer than necessary and can affect how you feel or perform. For example, if your friend tells you that they're going out with other friends, it is likely to make you feel that you are missing out and you will develop resentment over the fact that you are revising. It will be on your mind during revision and your concentration levels will be poor. Equally, if your friend tells you that they've been revising for a longer period than you, you'll feel that you are under performing which will make you feel upset when in actual fact you're performing very well, but now feel defeated. You don't know which direction the conversation will go so it is not recommended that you chance it.

### 3. Drinking Sugary Drinks

Avoid sugary drinks during the break time because this will cause your sugar to spike and then plummet, causing you to become sluggish and demotivated. You will lose focus and concentration, resulting in a very poor revision session. Don't avoid sugar at all costs, just avoid excess sugar which is often found in things like sweets, cakes and sugary, soda drinks. Regular consumption of sugary drinks will often lead to cravings for other foods and then the vicious cycle begins. The trick is to have a good breakfast that will sustain your energy throughout the day and if you have to have a snack have a piece of fruit such as a banana. That will help sustain sugar levels, but also provide you with valuable nutrients to support your brain and revision.

### 4. Screen-time and Social Media

It is important to try to avoid screen time during your break because this will distract your brain from processing information that it has just been fed. Screen-time over stimulates the brain and - depending on what you're doing - can cause you to lose track of time and put things off. Games are fun, but addictive and before you know it you will lose two or three hours of valuable revision time, during what was originally a half hour break. Your whole revision plan will be thrown off and something will have to be sacrificed to make back the time. Screen time doesn't often mean gaming, simple things like online video platforms can consume your time, because they are short and continuous and you often get stuck in a loop, where you are compelled to watch the next recommended video. Although the short online videos do have their place and are often entertaining, save it for a time when you know you can afford to relax, such as on a timetabled day off, when you will most definitely deserve it!

### 5. Going to Sleep
Although going to sleep does have its benefits, as mentioned previously, it is not recommended that you sleep between revision sessions. This is because you will not feel the full benefits of a good night's sleep and you'll feel tired, sluggish and unfocused. Try to maintain your energy with food, hydration and fresh air. If you do feel tired, make sure that you schedule enough sleep in the night to provide your brain with the opportunity to replenish and organise the information that it has encountered during the day. You will feel better and more refreshed for it and will always feel ready and prepared for revision.

## The Importance of Timetabling a Day Off

Believe it or not, it's actually quite important to timetable a day off for yourself, to do whatever it is you want to do. The benefits of a day off are that it is nice to have something to look forward to: it is like a goal or a treat. You can make plans to go out with your friends and look forward to it, knowing that you are not restricted by time. You will appreciate it more knowing that you worked hard during that week and can now enjoy the luxuries and rewards that it brings. Try not to discuss work with your friends because this is your time to rest and focus on yourself. However, it is important that you don't go overboard, otherwise it will set a negative tone for the start of the next revision week. For example, you don't want to stay out too late on your day off, otherwise your brain will not get its required amount of rest; equally, you shouldn't fill up on junk food, otherwise you'll feel sluggish and bloated which will affect you the following day. Remember, if you respect your body and brain it will pay you back.

Calming activities, such as going out with friends or visiting family members, or, perhaps going out for a meal, are good examples of how you could take it easy, but still maintain some kind of structure and organisation to your day, without bombarding your brain with over stimulation. However, it is important to avoid opting to have a lie-in on your day off and wasting your day vegging out - this will lead to poor habits and throw out your routine. It is essential to keep the engine running and the fuel flowing, in order to keep it well-conditioned. After all, a fit body is a fit mind.

## Mindfulness

It seems very apt during this work heavy time that we should explore the positive benefits of mindfulness and its application in preparing mentally for the stress of everyday life, as well as exams and exam preparation. Mindfulness can be a powerful tool in organising your thoughts and resetting your mind to focus on the task at hand. Everyday people practise mindfulness to maintain a healthy sense of balance and awareness. Schools and universities often encourage students to explore the benefits of mindfulness because of its positive effects on combating stress and anxiety, so it seems to make sense that during this stressful and high intensity period of your school career, incorporating mindfulness activities will promote better well-being and mental health.

So, what is mindfulness? Mindfulness can be described as being more aware of the 'here and now' and not focusing on past issues or future concerns. By focusing on the 'here and now' you are able to narrow your thought process to your immediate surroundings, focusing your concentration on the task in hand without outside distractions or disturbances. You can practise mindfulness in everyday life during everyday activities and it will make you feel less anxious and more positive

You will be forgiven for thinking that mindfulness involves simply sitting isolated in a room, cross legged, surrounded by scented candles, although that does sound quite tranquil. However, you would not be alone; this is a common misconception. The truth is that mindfulness can be practised anywhere and by anyone at any time of the day, although the quieter and more peaceful the surroundings, the better.

The benefits of mindfulness are quite simple and obvious. If you take time out of your day to practise mindfulness, or promote mindfulness during everyday activities such as eating, writing, drawing or whilst walking, you'll recognise that your focus is not split and your thoughts are not as chaotic. You are able to organise your thoughts and feel more positive and happier with your present situation. There is no point dwelling on the past and worrying about the future is a bit of a waste of time, because it can always change. The present is what matters, so make it count.

However, there are a few possible issues and anticipated problems in relation to practising mindfulness. To practise mindfulness effectively you'll need to limit your distractions, although a lot of these can be controlled by yourself; you are also relying on others to respect your time and provide you with the necessary environment, required to engage in mindfulness. Try to plan a convenient time and place to promote mindfulness where distractions are limited. If this space is not available in your house or learning environment, take time out to go for a walk and use this opportunity to practise mindfulness in an outdoor setting, where you will also benefit from fresh air.

So how do you apply mindfulness in a revision setting? What do you have to do to ensure that you are being mindful? Mindfulness is about thinking about the present, so use your current setting to think in detail about what it is you are doing at that time. For example, if you are writing, think about how the pen feels in your hand. Is it soft or is it hard? How does the pen feel when you're writing? Does it write smoothly? Can you feel the friction of the nib against the paper? Does it glide? How does it feel when you write neatly? Are you comfortable? How does the seat feel? Is it comfortable? Where are your feet resting? How does that feel? Which part of your feet are contacting the floor? Does the floor feel warm? These are just a few things you can think about when practising mindfulness in a revision situation.

Each of these questions forces you to think about your present situation. You are effectively analysing yourself in different ways. By doing this you are decluttering your thought process of any worries, concerns or upcoming events that will divide your focus and are likely to make you less effective when revising. You will feel more positive and more prepared, if you can schedule mindfulness activities into your everyday life. This book isn't about mindfulness, but there are plenty of resources online that you can use to become more familiar with mindfulness and how it can be applied to your life.

In conclusion, mindfulness is an effective tool to have in your arsenal to help prepare mentally for the challenge of revision and exams. It is quite a common practise and can be used to combat stress and anxiety in everyday situations. To practise mindfulness effectively, you do have to make sure that you are in the correct environment with limited distractions, otherwise your thought process will be distracted and cluttered with information that will hinder your efforts. The best part about mindfulness is that it can be practised by anybody, at any time of the day and it is entirely free, so why not give it a try. It will not cost you anything, but a few minutes of your time. The benefits will far outweigh the losses and you will feel more positive, focused and refreshed.

**Planned Worry Periods**

In this section we will discuss how to manage worry, which will creep in at some stage during the revision process or during exams. If you are somebody that worries a lot, this will help you to minimise this unwanted stress and feel more positive about your revision progress and your exam performance. Worry has a massive negative impact on your mental preparation during revision for your exams. This section will explore some ideas that have proven to be effective in managing anxiety, stress and worry and will explain how you can take control.

We have all worried at some stage for some reason, but what actually is worry and what can we do to prevent it? Worry is like a negative seed that develops and grows at a fast rate. Small worries, if not managed, will fester and eventually become huge concerns, mainly because you have provided the initial worry the time and opportunity to manifest. Worries don't have to be huge and often; whatever it was you were initially concerned about, in hindsight, often turns out to be a pointless waste of time anyway!

Worry can really impact some people whereas others just don't seem to be phased. The reality is that worrying can impact health negatively in several ways. Simple worries can escalate to anger, frustration, depression, lack of sleep or upset, which will all impact your performance in everyday life and not just on your revision. How can anyone focus effectively if they are fuelled with anger or if they haven't slept? The truth is, they won't.

Personally, I am a worrier and I look with great envy at those who take worries in their stride. How do they do it? Don't they care? The truth is, yes, they do, they just don't give the worry the legs to run and develop into the beast that consumes so many. After all, nothing positive would come from it, so what would be the point? So, what do they do, that we don't? Having spoken to a few, the attitude is the same. They actually do worry, but only for a very short time, a few minutes... that's it. It's what I have come to know or describe as 'planned worry time'.

Whether they knew about planned worry time or not is irrelevant, but they seem happier and more positive individuals because of it. So, what is planned worry time and what are the benefits? How can you apply planned worry time into your day? Planned worry time can be best described as a limited amount of time dedicated solely to possible issues or concerns. If you took five minutes at the beginning of everyday to get your worries out, it would then provide you with more time to focus on the job in hand. Sometimes you can discuss your worries with someone you trust because often they have had the same or similar worries at some stage. Perhaps prioritise your worries to create perspective, but why suffer in silence? After all, they say a problem shared is a problem halved. The key thing is to make sure that you don't give too much time to your worries otherwise they will fester. If practised regularly, you will also be able to appear very relaxed and controlled.

The benefits of planning worry time are vast and all link to a better sense of well-being and increased productivity. It seems quite obvious, but if you are not worrying about problems or issues, then it would be fair to say that you have quite a good sense of well-being. It is nice to have few concerns and puts you into a more positive mind-set. As you get older, your worries will increase, but as long as these are managed you will lead a more positive and happier life. You often hear people say I wish I could sleep like I did when I was a baby, or I wish I could be a child again and this is often because there was little responsibility and lack of serious concern that impacted life and decision-making at a young age. Unfortunately, those stresses can't be avoided as people age and responsibility increases, but they can be managed.

It would seem to make more sense to pre-empt the potential worry and put measures in place to minimise or dampen the effect, as opposed to wait for the worry to happen and address it when it's too late. During revision time and exams, often individuals will worry if they are under prepared or the individuals are poorly managed and these are things that are easily preventable. As mentioned previously, organising a revision timetable and plotting a realistic time frame can help prevent a lot of the worry leading up to exams and during the actual assessments themselves. If you know that you have prepared thoroughly and have revised the content for your exam, why would you worry? It is natural to feel a little bit anxious, but the trick is that as long as you plan and prepare you will feel confident and ready for the challenge of the exam.

In conclusion, it is fair to say that everybody worries at some stage and some people's worries seem quite trivial in comparison to others. Worry can have a serious impact on your mental well-being and can lead to anger frustration, depression, lack of sleep and upset, which will all impact your performance leading up to and during your exams. Worry can be managed effectively using 'planned worry time'. If you give worry the legs to run, it will race out of control and consume you. You can try to share your worries with someone else or you can write them all down and give them only a limited amount of your day, so that you can focus on the task in hand. It is a skill to manage your worries, but it makes more sense to prevent the worry happening in the first instance. Make sure that you are organised and follow a realistic plan and time schedule to eliminate the possibility of anxiety and worry and feel more confident in preparation for your exams.

In summary, there is a lot of overlap between mental and physical preparation, but what is consistent across both is that they complement each other in making sure that you are performing at the highest level. It is important to stick to a routine that is achievable. It is easy to say that you will go home and do four hours of revision but that is just not practical, and even if you are able to sustain four hours straight revising, how effective has it really been? Are you retaining the information or just kidding yourself? Routine is key when trying to ensure you perform at your best. Set achievable goals with realistic targets, and slowly but positively and productively, work to achieve them.

# Chapter 4: Don't Let Invaders Infiltrate Your Base!

So, we have discussed mental and physical preparation for revision in good detail, without going all 'sciencey' but we've covered a lot of ground nonetheless. In this section we need to discuss your immediate environment and what you can do to make sure that it is set in the most organised and effective way. You need to be in a position where you are always ready to revise, so that you are in the correct mind-set and have no organisation or preparation issues. Poor environmental organisation is likely to cause you to procrastinate and put you off making a good positive start on the task in hand.

## The Importance of a Consistent Base

Having a consistent base to revise is important because you know it is always prepared and you can start revision straightaway; you know it is readily accessible and forms the cornerstone of a consistent work ethic. If your base is inconsistent and continuously moves around to different rooms or different surfaces, it will make revision difficult as there is no consistency and ultimately it will affect the quality of your study time. It also opens up the possibility of becoming distracted as different environments are accessible by other people or pets. It is essential that you establish your own revision base and make sure that it remains the same throughout the revision process.

## Cluttered Space is a Cluttered Mind

To maintain an organised, clutter-free base is an important part of an effective and efficient revision protocol. It is essential that the resources you use are prepared in an organised fashion and easy to access. If your immediate environment is cluttered, it will ultimately bleed into your revision and output, meaning that you will not be able to focus or revise effectively, especially if you're constantly looking for resources and are trying to work in cramped, cluttered conditions. Your brain will be focused elsewhere and very little work will be completed. Remember a cluttered space is a cluttered mind. It is for that reason that you must ensure that your revision base is clutter free and organised, eliminating any possible potential distractions.

Distractions such as the TV or music will hinder the revision process because it will be inevitable at some stage that you'll be focusing more on the background noise than the revision. A particular song may take your fancy, or something on TV may peak your interest. Those who claim that listening to music helps them revise, are only kidding themselves. For example, how many times have you read the page of the book, magazine or webpage and then had to re-read it and then re-read it again because you didn't take in any information? It looks like you're reading as you're looking down at the article, but your brain has been divided and your attention is elsewhere. It is essential therefore, that when you revise, you need to minimise the distractions to make sure your only focus is the revision and it has your undivided attention.

It is essential that you practice working in a limited environment. Remember, you are preparing for an exam and in an exam situation you'll have a table, chair, basic stationery, the exam paper and maybe a bottle of water. Working in this type of environment at home will prepare you mentally for the challenge of the exam. The exam situation will come more naturally to you and you will feel comfortable in the environment, which in turn will make you feel relaxed and ready for the challenge. Sometimes sitting in a hall in silence can feel uncomfortable if you haven't done it before. The magnitude of the exam becomes greater and the pressure will affect your performance. Think smart, create the perfect environment and get into the appropriate mind-set.

So what types of things do you have at your revision base? As this is not an exam, you can have a little bit more, but remember too much is just clutter. So, here are a list of things that you must have in your revision base to ensure you get the most out of each session.

## Things to Have in Your Base

Firstly, it seems very obvious, but it is essential, that you work on a flat surface. Working on your bed, on your lap or on the edge of the couch are not ideal surfaces to do the best revision. It does not set the right tone and does not provide you with conditions similar to that of an exam. It will, in effect, provide you with a false perspective. In addition, anything you write is not going to be its neatest if the surface is uneven. Afterall, what good are revision notes, if you can't read them?

Next on the list of essential things at your revision base is a study chair. It is crucial that you have a suitable chair to sit on during your revision. You don't want to waste time and energy on a rickety old stool, with uneven legs, as you want to direct full concentration to the revision, not on the little irritations that will ultimately become bigger distractions. Try to avoid swivel chairs as this will also slowly become another big distraction.

Remember, you are trying to replicate an exam style environment to prepare you mentally for the challenge ahead. I can assure you that you will not have the choice of sitting on your bed or spinning on a chair in your exam.

Another essential for your revision base is a selection of basic stationery. This should consist of a pen, pencil, rubber, ruler, selection of highlighters, maths equipment, sticky notes and a notebook. These things should be easily organised in a simple revision base and don't forget that you also have the resource material that you'll be revising from among this basic equipment. Try to have a bin at hand so you don't generate a lot of paper waste which will cause clutter. Spare equipment can be kept out of the way during revision to keep things as simple and clean as possible. Should a pen run out or pencil not sharpen, you can always dip into the supplies and replace it - this will eliminate the need for you to eat too much into your revision time.

Post-it Notes or sticky notes are essential during this time because they are a great way to document ideas and synthesise information, which I will be going through in more detail later on. If seventeen years of teaching has taught me anything, it's that Post-it Notes are versatile and can be used to maximum effect during the revision process. My advice has always been that, if you can synthesise a page of information onto a Post-it Note, then you are producing a range of excellent revision resources.

Water is a must at any revision base to keep you hydrated and keep your brain functioning at the highest possible level. Having water at hand, will prevent you from leaving your base to go and look for water or an alternative. A simple water bottle is more than enough to keep you hydrated and fresh. Keep it simple, avoid sugary drinks or drinks with additives as mentioned previously and drink water as a main source of hydration.

Finally, having a notepad in your revision base is a welcome addition because it can be used to scribble ideas or doodle your thoughts and support in the synthesis of your ideas, into an effective set of revision notes. It is important not to believe that you have to fill the notebook from front to back, to have effective revision notes. Although that will work for some people, it is not the most efficient and effective way to revise. More concentration will be going into making your handwriting neat and filling the page as opposed to the quality of revision taking place. You could fall into the trap of many, by basing the success of your revision on the quantity of notes and not the quality.

**Top Things to Avoid**

It is important that your revision base is not in the main flow of your house and is neatly tucked away for maximum privacy. However, sometimes your revision base could be invaded and measures need to be taken to ensure that a possible invasion is avoided. This will ensure you can spend quality time revising in a quiet private environment.

Among the numerous possible invaders, one in particular is pets. There is nothing wrong in owning a pet and taking time out to play with your pet has actually proven to help relaxation and combat stress. However, pets can sometimes be unpredictable and will climb and settle in the most unusual places. As entertaining as this may be on a regular day, having Mr Fluffy settle on your revision notes and refusing to shift without a fight is not going to be helpful or support your goals and targets. It is recommended that pets are kept out of your revision base, so that your routine is not disturbed and your revision is effective.

Family are also considered invaders. Family members are not likely to sit on your revision notes like Mr Fluffy, but family members can also be unpredictable, often entering your room unannounced or asking questions that take away from your concentration and revision time. Simple things, like making your family aware of your timetable or putting a sign on your door will help others to understand your plan and respectfully let them know that you are currently unavailable. I am sure that your family will respect your wishes and understand that you are trying hard to achieve your goals. It might also be an idea that you ask your family in advance what the plans are for the week and try to establish a consistent time in the evening for your dinner so that you can plan around it.

In summary, your revision base is equally as important as your mental and physical preparation in the lead up to your exams. Preparing your environment in an organised fashion will help you become more organised and feel ready and more positive for the challenge. Avoiding clutter and using the bare minimum equipment required will help you focus more effectively and efficiently on the main goal of revising for your exams and retaining information. Remember, a cluttered environment is a cluttered mind. Making family members aware of your plan and timetable will ensure that your time is spent without disruption or disturbance and ensuring your revision base is out of the main flow of the house will provide you with the best opportunity and best environment to revise comfortably in preparation for exams. You just have to find a way to communicate this to Mr Fluffy, without a fight.

# Chapter 5: Revising with Sprinkles and Buttercream!

In theory, most revision techniques - if not all revision techniques - are likely to be effective in some way or another, but instead of me publishing a book of 1000 techniques and asking you to spend hours, if not days, deciding which one is best for you (essentially wasting your time), I have decided, using my years of experience, to provide you with the bare essentials that are the foundation of all of the revision techniques. These include: how to skim and scan a text; how to identify key ideas within a text; and, how to synthesise this information into a powerful revision note that you can use to refer back to very quickly, instead of re-reading an entire exercise book. I will make this as easy as possible to interpret and understand because I recognise that time is of the essence. I will use every day examples to demonstrate exactly how to apply these principles effectively so that you can recognise these opportunities in your revision. It will take a little bit of practice at first, but I assure you, the process will be natural very quickly and you will wish that you'd been doing this for years. You'll be impressed with how easy it is to retain information and recall facts with these.

All revision techniques involve the same fundamentals: you often revisit information, skim it or scan it, identify key ideas and then synthesise it into a format that can be easily digested. This is ultimately what revision is in simple terms. Different revision techniques are just different ways of rebranding these fundamentals. The issue is that the essentials can often be lost in the method or gimmick and revision, although varied and interesting, is often not effective or efficient. Therefore, I will strip it back to the absolute basics, so that you can apply these effectively in your own revision plan.

### Skimming for Key Facts and Figures?

So, what is skimming and why is it important? Skimming involves quickly identifying things that stand out, like facts and figures. What they mean, isn't important at first, as you are just pulling out bits of information that appear significant at a glance.

The benefits of skimming are that you start your revision process off with a bang. You jump in and start gathering information without heavy reading or vast note taking. Skimming information is an easy and effective way to re-familiarise yourself with key points and key facts. These key points and key facts are like sprinkles on a cake, they are everywhere in a text and they make a difference to the overall presentation. You are not reading, but looking for things that standout, as if you were looking for a letter in a word search. If it pops or jumps off a page, it is likely to have significance and can be a pivotal point to base your key ideas around. For example, if I wrote the date 1066, without adding any further information or context (it's the Battle of Hastings), your mind starts to rummage through its mental filing cabinet to add context. Your mind is recalling previously learned information in order to fill the voids. It is surprising what you know when presented with simple facts and figures. You are essentially building a story around a small snippet of information. Remember, you are skimming not reading, there's a difference.

**Scanning for Context**

Skimming is a great way to identify significant facts and figures that appear in a text and often reignite buried knowledge that you have learned previously. However, what happens if these facts and figures don't reignite previously learned knowledge? That's when we begin to scan the text and begin to add context manually. You will not be reading the text from top to bottom but will instead read around the facts to try and build a bigger picture and understand the significance of the information that you have skimmed.

Scanning is another effective revision technique because it can also be done quickly and easily. Skimming and scanning combined can help you read through a text at a greater speed, which will save you time, effort and energy. Sometimes, all it may take is skimming and scanning and you might feel satisfied that you have the general idea of the content of the page. However, to ensure that your revision is effective, carry on with the process and don't cut corners because cutting corners is only going to give you a false perspective.

Hopefully you can now see a pattern emerging. You start off with the basics, (skimming), and then gradually add meat (scanning) to the bones until your revision notes are full of important content, but have been carefully crafted to include minimal but impactful information that includes key facts. If skimming is seen as the sprinkles of the cake, then scanning is the butter cream that the sprinkles are sitting on. They don't form the body of the cake but add the colour and character and without them the cake would be boring and bland. (I think my cake example is working well).

The next stage in the process is to build on the skimming and scanning and develop key ideas that will begin to form the body of the revision.

# Chapter 6: Identifying Key Ideas to Give Body to the Cake

At the moment you have two tools that you can use to quickly identify key information and form a basic idea based on recall. You also have a basic technique to use if you are unable to recall information. These techniques can be used individually or together and can be effective, depending on the type of information you are revising. However, I find that they work most effective as part of this particular system as you are able to review a text from different perspectives and become familiar with the context. To add more substance to these revision notes, we will now need to review the text and use the facts or figures to help generate key ideas. A key idea is an overall picture based on and including facts and figures. It consists of two lines of information that you have summarised from a paragraph. What makes these two lines important is that they consist of information that you generated through the skimming and scanning. This is why it is important to follow the whole process because slowly you build a stronger and more solid set of revision notes in very few words.

## Revision Based Scenario

So, let's imagine that you need to revise a page that consists of six paragraphs of text. How would you tackle this?

In preparation and to save time, draw four vertical columns in your notebook with the headings: skimming, scanning, key ideas and synthesis (the latter will be explained in the next chapter).

1. To begin the process, quickly skim the entire page and list any key facts and figures into the skimming column in your notebook; this might consist of individual words or dates that seem significant. If it jumps out, write it down or if it's easier, draw a picture or doodle. Don't spend too much time skimming, it is meant to be fast.

2. The next step is to begin scanning to add context to these facts and figures by reading around them and writing down what these key facts and figures mean - in the scanning column. Try to use few words and keep it concise! You could draw a picture that tells a story, if that is your preferred learning style.

3. The next part of this process involves you reading one paragraph at a time and summarising that

paragraph to no more than two lines, but try to use as many key facts and figures as you can. The two lines that you generate are called key ideas and form the basis of what that paragraph is about. These lines will be written in the key ideas column in your notebook. However, instead of copying down the entire page as 'revision notes', you have summarised each paragraph into no more than two lines, which means your six-paragraph page of text has become 12 lines of quality revision notes. You can understand now, using the cake example, how the key ideas form the body, the scanning the buttercream topping, and the skimming the sprinkles.

There are different ways that you can record this information. You can write your key ideas down using normal everyday handwriting or you could try and communicate the key ideas in a doodle or drawing. Ultimately, how you develop your key ideas is down to you and your preferred learning style. It's about refreshing your knowledge and being able to recall necessary information when you need it. Nobody will come to your house and tell you your revision is wrong.

In summary, skimming, scanning and developing key ideas are the fundamentals of any revision method or process. Identifying key facts and adding context and then presenting these in the form of sentences helps you to slowly build a solid set of revision notes. This process can be further developed, with the use of synthesis which will help you to condense your key ideas into a more economic form, that can be used as flashcards and encourage information recall. Your revision notes are specific to you, they are for you and you understand them, that's all that matters. Don't let anyone else devalue or criticise your revision strategy, just because it is different to theirs.

# Chapter 7: How to Create Simple Revision Notes

We have learned the value of skimming a text and have developed a good understanding of how to add context to facts and figures. We have developed this information into key ideas which consist of one or two sentences to summarise each paragraph, specifically including the facts, figures and contextual supporting information. The next thing is synthesis. So, what is synthesis and what are the benefits?

Synthesis, in simple terms, is taking all of the information available and stripping it down to what is essential, but not taking away from the important content. This can be presented in the form of a concise paragraph. To use the cake example again, synthesis is like the box that the cake is in, presenting the cake as a compact package in its full glory.

The benefits of synthesising information are that you can combine ideas to form a small piece of well-informed writing. Synthesising your key ideas into a paragraph will produce a very concise revision note that can be referred to prior to an exam to keep knowledge fresh. However, having already approached your text from different perspectives and having analysed it in different ways, you should have a good understanding of the topic anyway, this will just reinforce it.

Use the final column in your notebook, titled synthesis, to write down your paragraph based on the information in your key ideas, which should be laid out clearly in the third column. You can use this opportunity to further simplify your key ideas, to make all of the sentences flow together into one continuous paragraph. This process helps you decipher what information is important and what information can be side-lined. The clever part is that, for you to make this decision, you will inevitably read the information several times to make sure it is concise and flows, thus further embedding the knowledge you have acquired.

You can't leave this information in your notebook as that would be impractical, so you now need to start to produce revision flashcards or Post-it Notes. Flashcards are a good way to keep information compact and concise and can easily be carried around to revise on the go. Flashcards should not really exceed the size of your hand because the information included should not be a complete copy of your original notes, but a synthesised compact version that is easy to understand and process. Also, if you are restricted to a small space to write your notes, you'll become an expert in filtering quality information from a text. The process will get easier and your revision notes will become, more and more concise.

**Chunking**

It is important to recognise that there are different ways to analyse a text and synthesise information. 'Chunking' is a method that you can use to synthesise information and break it down into easy to process 'chunks'. There are several different ways to synthesise information to make it easier to recall. We will address some of these, but first we will start by addressing 'chunking'. 'Chunking' is often used in education to break down large quantities of information into smaller more manageable nuggets of knowledge that can be processed easily. When put together, these small nuggets of knowledge form a bigger picture, which will come together easier in the form of 'chunks' as opposed to trying to take large quantities of information in straight off the bat.

'Chunking', in simple terms, is breaking a large piece of text into digestible sections. The smaller sections could be broken into concise paragraphs or sentences. Breaking this information into smaller paragraphs or more manageable sentences means that you can analyse and scrutinise the information, without feeling overwhelmed with the large quantity of information, originally presented to you. It is essentially splitting things up.

'Chunking' can prove quite effective when synthesising information because you can break your key ideas into two smaller easy to process sentences as opposed to one large difficult to process paragraph. It does depend on the type of information you are trying to synthesise because sometimes one paragraph might be perfect, whereas a piece of text that is dense with facts, figures and information might be easier to process if you break it into smaller 'chunks'.

The benefits of 'chunking' are that the information has been broken down into easy to process 'chunks'. If this information has been broken down, it should be easier to process. It effectively provides you with a greater opportunity to retain information and recall it when required. For example, 'chunking' works effectively when analysing extended pieces of writing or pages of text. If you were to break down a piece of text into four sections and analyse each section in isolation, you will slowly begin to identify key points and key ideas that will help form the bigger picture. When you review each chunk, the bigger picture will be revealed, like a jigsaw, which will then begin to unlock other ideas that perhaps would not be at the forefront of your mind due to the large amount of information initially provided.

However, although 'chunking' is a very effective way of breaking information down so that you can process it at a faster rate, it can be quite time-consuming, especially if you are trying to 'chunk' large pieces of text and analyse them in forensic detail. If this is a process you intend to adopt during your revision sessions, then it might be worth planning your timetable to accommodate for the extra time that it will take for you to 'chunk' a text and slowly process it. Another alternative would be to give yourself a fixed amount of time per page of information, or per paragraph, to make sure that you stick to your revision timetable.

In summary, 'chunking' is a really effective way of breaking down large pieces of text into simple components that can be easily analysed and processed. 'Chunking' is also an easy way of presenting information while synthesising your key ideas so that you don't have to quickly read over extensive synthesised notes prior to your exams. 'Chunking' the information into manageable sizes makes it so much easier to digest and process. However, the process can take time so serious consideration needs to go into how you effectively arrange your revision timetable to accommodate for the additional time that you may need. 'Chunking' isn't always appropriate but is an effective way to break down texts. It might be worth noting, whilst preparing for exams that involve facts and formulae, there are other more effective ways to synthesise information such as the use of acronyms.

## Acronyms and Mnemonics

An acronym is a short, sharp and creative method of presenting information in an easy to process, quick and fun context. It is important to explore a range of processes because it will add variety to your revision, but also be a refreshing change to the routine. We must first explore what an acronym is and how they can be a fun part of the revision process. If information is seen to be more fun or entertaining, it is more likely to be retained and recalled in an exam.

In simple terms, an acronym is an abbreviation using the initial letters of words to form another word. We all use acronyms on a daily basis, for example LOL is an acronym of laugh out loud. We have all come to the common understanding that LOL is used to signify that something is funny or amusing. You can apply this idea to things such as rules or laws or remembering artefacts or planets. For example, 'ROY G BIV' is an acronym of the colours of the rainbow in order: Red, Orange, Yellow, Blue, Indigo and Violet. On the other hand, mnemonics, are unusual, sometimes rhythmic, little coded sentences, which act as memory joggers. For example, a mnemonic that I learned in primary school, 'My Very Energetic Mother, Just Swam Under North Pole', is a mnemonic for the planets in the solar system, in order of closest to the sun: Mercury, Venus, Earth, Mars, Jupiter, Saturn, Uranus, Neptune and Pluto. The reason I am able to recall this information is because of the somewhat strange but easy to remember imaginary event involving my energetic mother, who swam under the North Pole. Using acronyms and mnemonics must be effective, because I learned that mnemonic thirty-five years ago and I'm able to recall it with ease.

If, for example, you are trying to revise the table of elements, it might be worth creating a mnemonic for each row. It is far easier to remember a fun mnemonic rather than try to memorise the rows of the table of elements cold. The more fun and bizarre the better, because it makes them easier to recall and they act like 'memory joggers'. It's a bit like listening to a song on the radio - without trying, you'll soon know the lyrics. You didn't learn them, you didn't intend to learn them, but after a while you seem to just be singing along. It's because the song has rhythm and repetition and is interesting, similar to a mnemonic. Mnemonics are a good way to memorise muscle groups, the human skeleton or the digestive system and so on. If you're feeling really creative, why not turn your mnemonic into a song! It will make your revision fun and varied but also have value. The best part is, a quick internet image search demonstrates that there are pre-existing mnemonics waiting for you to use! Using search terms like 'science mnemonics', will save you time and also support your revision.

In summary, it is good to vary your revision and identify ways to make the process fun and stimulating but still have value. It is so easy to get stuck in a rut during this process because there is lack of variety in what you are doing, which can be monotonous. Incorporating a range of techniques through the use of acronyms, mnemonics, poems or little songs, helps create variation and breaks up the routine. Acronyms have become part of our everyday life and for good reason. Acronyms are easier to write and remember, because they are in an abbreviated form and it is much quicker when texting or messaging. Mnemonics are helpful because they aid you in visualising a story or event and help jog your memory. So, it makes sense that we should take advantage of these little gifts and apply them to the revision process because it is something that we are already familiar with and can apply so easily to our revision.

**Explaining to Someone Else**
There will ultimately come a point in your revision process when somebody asks, "So, how's the revision going?" This opens up the opportunity for dialogue, where you can explain exactly what you have learned during that particular revision session. Take full advantage of this, because although they are probably just asking out of politeness, it is a great opportunity for you to run through exactly what you have learned and recap verbally what you have done. You could run through the key ideas that you've generated based on a text, or you can verbalise what you have synthesised.

Explaining things to someone else is a good way to practise your recall and develop confidence in yourself and your revision techniques. This conversation could develop into an interesting two-way discussion, where the person you're talking to might add little bits of additional supporting information to what you already know. This will then give you the opportunity to broaden your knowledge and further develop your understanding, ultimately making you feel more prepared and ready for your exams. Adding a discussion to your study plan also creates 'layers' to your revision which supports your ability to retain and recall information and also adds variety to the process.

Feeling confident in your ability will also give you the confidence to actively participate in class discussion, without feeling underprepared or self-conscious. Actively engaging in class dialogue opens up further opportunities to share information and continue to add to the layers of revision. Do you have to get involved in discussion? Although you can revise successfully without getting involved in conversation, it is a good way to mix up your current revision protocol, yet continue to add to your ever-growing bank of knowledge. You can revise very successfully without discussion, but adding variety can be refreshing.

Discussing your revision, whether it be with an individual or as part of a group, is also beneficial as it can highlight gaps or weaknesses in your knowledge. Identifying these gaps will give you the opportunity to independently seek out the correct information and add it to your revision notes. It can be disheartening not having the answers or being incorrect, especially if you spent two hours revising a topic. However, it is better to identify the gaps early as opposed to on the exam day. It is also important not to beat yourself up or feel that your revision is not effective because you have highlighted a gap. Get into the habit of seeing it more as an opportunity rather than a failing. Gaps are there to be filled! Be positive.

In summary, discussing your revision with somebody opens many doors. It provides opportunities to test your knowledge retention and recall, while also helping to identify gaps or weaknesses that can be filled. Actively participating in discussion with an individual or a group will make you feel more confident with your knowledge and provide you with the environment to listen and share knowledge. This will ultimately add layers to your revision, constantly adding to and building upon the foundations that you have already put in place. Although it is not essential to have a discussion to support your revision, it's always good to add variety to keep the revision process interesting and productive.

Synthesis is a good way of condensing facts and figures with thoughts and ideas, into one informative piece of writing. Synthesising information helps to improve your ability to decipher important information from that which may not be as useful, resulting in better quality revision notes in fewer words. Revision isn't about copying out your existing workbook in neat, but instead about identifying the key points and key ideas in a text or document and taking away the most important parts to be used in an exam situation. Undertaking this process will help you realise that actually revision isn't that difficult or time-consuming. You will realise how easy it is to re-familiarise yourself with a range of topics using some very simple techniques.

# Chapter 8: The Method in Simple Terms

In this section we will look at the revision process as explained previously, in very simple terms. This is because, you have either arrived at this point of the book naturally and want to see the process in its simplest form, to clarify and solidify everything that you have just read, or, you have skipped ahead, looking for the easiest possible solution, bypassing a lot of other essential information, probably because you have not prepared very well and are in a desperate state. If this is the case, then the process will work for you also, but remember, poor planning, leads to poor performance.

In basic form, the process is: skimming, scanning, key ideas and synthesis. That's it! It looks easy and straightforward, because it is easy and straightforward. These are the fundamentals of any revision technique and you will find revision a lot more straightforward and a more valuable use of your time, if you adopt this technique in its basic form and apply it to your own revision. Each step of the process builds on the previous step. This is beneficial for so many reasons, but to keep it simple, you are constantly reviewing information in many different ways and it will stick.

These ideas should be written in your notebook in the suggested columns and kept safe to refer back to, should you ever want to access or add to them. It might be an idea to have a notebook specific to each subject, at least then you will know exactly where to find information should you require it. It is much easier to revise from a condensed form of your exercise books prior to an exam, as opposed to revising your entire collection of exercise books, which is hugely inefficient and totally impractical. You will be surprised how much knowledge you have actually absorbed during the course of your qualification that does not have to be written down. It has merely been reignited having seen triggers such as facts or figures; your brain fills in the blanks.

The reality is that without realising, we follow this format of processing every day; this process is not new but just been formalised and presented in an easy to apply format. To demonstrate this, in the next section I will apply this technique to everyday scenarios and demonstrate how this technique is naturally applied to your everyday life in any given scenario.

# Chapter 9: Everyday Examples

In this section I'm going to demonstrate to you how you apply skimming, scanning, key ideas and synthesis in everyday, real life scenarios and you'll see how it works for you there so technically it has to work for your revision too. So, let's move forward and see how this technique is actually used in everyday life.

**Scenario 1.**
Scenario one will be based in a restaurant. Imagine that you are looking at the menu that consists of about ten pages. When you sit at a restaurant table and look at the menu, it is very rare that you will read that menu from the front to back and top to bottom. This is where skimming happens. When you are presented with the menu, you begin to skim the menu looking for things that you are familiar with, such as burgers. When you eventually find burgers listed on the menu, without realising it you begin to scan the information around those words to obtain a bit more information as to the flavour or the contents.

When you are satisfied with some of the selections you begin to look at them in more detail, after all you can only have one meal, so you try to acquire more information and develop key ideas. These key ideas are generated in the menu but also through the conversation that you might have with the waitress/waiter or those you are having a meal with. This will provide you with a better idea of what the meal is like and whether you are likely to enjoy it. The synthesis happens when you amalgamate this information down and place your order. This is a very basic but obvious example of how you can apply skimming, scanning, key ideas and synthesis to an everyday scenario. You have filtered a ten-page menu down to one meal, but along the way, read and processed a lot of other information to inform your decision.

**Scenario 2.**
Scenario two will be based on a football match. A football match lasts about ninety minutes, but there are a lot of things that will happen during that match. If you were asked if you watched the match last night, would you recite minute for minute details about what happened, or would you give a brief summary of things that stood out or interesting things that took place? The answer would be that you would provide a brief overview of things that stood out and interesting things that took place, but you might then tag on your own personal opinion as to what you thought of the

match overall. This is effectively you synthesising the football match.

## Skimming (Facts and figures)
The home team won 1-0, having scored a penalty in the sixty-ninth minute.

## Scanning (Adding context to the facts and figures)
The home team was lucky to win 1-0, as the penalty should not have been awarded. They scored in the sixty-ninth minute.

## Key Ideas (Summarising key moments)
The match was very eventful; both teams were evenly matched. The home team were lucky to win 1-0, as the penalty should not have been allowed. They scored in the sixty-ninth, but also had a goal disallowed for offside in the seventy-second minute. Overall, it was a very entertaining match.

The synthesis happens when you discuss this with your friend or family member and you are able to recall some of these key moments and engage in discussion. You don't write this information down, but you take it in naturally whilst watching the football match and recall key moments as the focus for discussion. For example, if I now present you with the date 1066, I don't need to tell you why it's significant. This is because it was mentioned earlier; you can recall this information using the 1066 trigger. This is what happens when you discuss a football match or event: key moments act as triggers.

# Chapter 10: Other Useful Easy Ideas

As a teacher, parents often ask me what their child could be doing to further improve the chances of achieving the best possible grades. My answers tend to be the same, so I will present to you several examples with reasons as to why I believe they are effective in preparing you for an exam and these should definitely be a significant part of your revision protocol.

It should be standard practice to use past papers as a good benchmark of your knowledge. Past papers should not just be seen as an activity that you might do at school and should be taken as a serious opportunity to test your knowledge as well as your ability to manage your time effectively in an exam scenario. Misreading an exam paper or mismanaging time during an exam are some of the key reasons some people don't achieve their full potential. Simple mistakes like this can be avoided through exam practise. There are plenty of past papers online for free and they can be found on the exam board's website. You can download these as PDF files and print them out. This is also helpful because sometimes you are able to identify common themes or trends and can use these to inform your revision. It is definitely excellent practice to use past papers to support your revision.

When completing past papers, it is essential that you do this under exam conditions, which means no distractions, limited resources and a clock to time your progress. A good way to manage your time is to first skim through the paper and identify those questions that carry the most marks. By completing these questions first, it will mean that you are already banking the lion's share of the marks and if you run out of time you are still likely to get an excellent grade because you approached the exam with a clear plan. Focusing too much time on questions offering one or two marks will mean that you don't give yourself enough time to attack the questions offering the most marks. Inevitably you will feel rushed and are likely to make a mistake.

It is also essential not to leave any questions blank because a blank answer gets zero marks. However, if you have a realistic guess, there's a chance that you could get something, however small. Imagine if you got two or three marks simply for producing a realistic guess. That could be the difference between an entire grade. So, if you are unsure or you don't know, always have a realistic guess. Sometimes it even pays to leave it blank until the end, because in some exams the answers can actually be on the paper. For example, I remember a French GCSE exam which asked you to translate a postcard as one of the first questions. Later on, in the same exam, it asked you to write a postcard to your family. Any smart person would recognise the opportunity straight away and use the postcard example from the early stage of the exam to inform the structure and content of their answer. Sometimes the answer is hidden in plain sight, you just have to learn to be patient, take your time and read the exam carefully. You will be surprised how much information is actually available in front of you.

**Exam Technique**
Exam technique is mentioned a lot by teachers and although a lot of what is mentioned above is considered 'exam technique', something that I have not yet addressed, is knowing exactly how to get the most marks when answering a question. You'll be surprised how many people simply just throw away marks because they don't read the question carefully and don't fulfil the criteria. Exam questions will have a mark allowance and it is essential that you provide an answer that is worth the marks on offer. For example, if the question is offering two marks, it requires two valid points that are well explained. However, often it is believed by some that only a

couple of words are required, which is either very lazy or a very ill-judged, badly thought out response. For example, in a Product Design exam, it may offer two marks to explain the benefits, of using oak for garden furniture. To use only a couple of words, *'durable and weather resistant',* is not enough to achieve the mark on offer. You would simply just be listing words, with no explanation and asking the examiner to fill in the blanks. You need to further explain your answer, in a sentence. For example:

*Oak is used in garden furniture because it is a hardwood that is long-lasting and durable. The robust nature of oak also makes it quite weather resistant.*

This is an example that would more than achieve the full marks on offer; it uses the same words, but includes a clear explanation. You can go onto any exam board website and find the corresponding mark scheme to any past paper.

Mark schemes are an excellent way to cross-reference your answers when practising for an exam. Often in the mark scheme it will provide you with several possible answers or points that would be considered valid as an answer to a particular question. It will also provide guidance to the person marking the exams as to exactly how many marks to award, based on the quality of the explanation. It is definitely worth developing your exam technique, practicing past papers and cross referencing your answers against the mark scheme. This will make you more aware of what a quality answer looks like, but also what the person marking your exam will be looking for in terms of justification.

# Chapter 11: Life-Long Learning

In this section we will be exploring the 'what if?' What if you don't do well in your exams? What if you don't get the grades you need? What if you don't get any qualifications at all? It would be fair to say there are a lot of questions and uncertainties. There is no guarantee that everyone who revises is going to get top grades, although it certainly increases your chances, but sometimes luck just isn't on your side. A simple mis-read of a question or mental block in an exam, can cost you a few marks, which could ultimately cost you a grade.

We will be looking at the options available to you after your exams, should things not go your way and what you can do, should you not succeed in achieving your desired results. We will explore pathways and opportunities available to you that don't rely on GCSEs and A-levels and also explore other ways in which you can further your education without having to re-sit GCSEs at school. It seems negative to explore the 'what if', but it can also be quite settling knowing that there are other options available.

Firstly, it is important to realise that if you don't get the grades that you wanted or you don't achieve any qualifications at all, you have to learn to forgive yourself. There is no point in looking back exploring the things you could've done differently because you'll be on a downward spiral of upset and regret. It is a very lonely journey with no real positive outcome. You have to learn to forgive yourself and move on. Life is long and full of opportunities and learning does not start and stop at school. Other learning opportunities are available outside of the school setting and you can actually sit qualifications independently away from a school or even online. A lot of people believe that, as they have 'outgrown school' or have 'gotten too old', the opportunity for education has passed and the only option available is to get a job and work. Although this option has its benefits and you can achieve great success working up in a company through the ranks, there are still other options available to you should you not achieve your full potential in school. As teachers, we call these pathways.

Pathways are routes to the next stage in your education. The pathway from GCSE could be to A-level and the pathway from A-level could be a foundation diploma and the pathway from the foundation diploma could be to do a degree. However, alternative pathways are also available. The pathway from GCSE could be to do an apprenticeship, while the pathway from apprenticeship could be to college or a job. Pathways vary depending on your intention. Therefore, it is important not to compare yourself to other people's successes. Other people don't have your goals and intentions; therefore, their goals and successes are different to yours. There is no comparison.

The glory is that, there is no fixed path or structure to learning and no deadline date as to when learning should stop. Learning can happen any time and not necessarily in an educational setting. If you want to achieve a bank of GCSEs, that option is always available whether you are 16 or 46. This also applies to any other qualification. This is called 'life-long learning', where every experience or adventure teaches you something new. Whether you develop invaluable experience that can be passed on to friends or colleagues or a skill, that will make you a more confident person or more employable; or, whether you want to focus on a subject or topic and work through qualifications, life is a learning experience, so enjoy it!

In summary, life is filled with many opportunities to learn and develop as a valuable, contributing member of society. Exams are one such pathway that provides you with a direction that is appropriate for some and not for others. It can be beneficial to get as many qualifications as you can because you will develop other transferable skills along the way. For example, you might not use algebraic equations again, on a routine basis, but if you can do them, you demonstrate excellent problem-solving skills. This is transferable across a range of potential career paths. Regardless of your pathway, recognise that learning is organic and can appear in many forms, not just questions on an exam paper or writing in a book. Whatever your option, appreciate that failure does exist and can sometimes be the learning experience. Embrace it, reconfigure, forgive yourself and carry on down the path – that's learning.

# Conclusion

In conclusion, you now have the tools, knowledge and skills to make effective revision notes in an easy to implement way to optimise your exam performance and achieve the best possible outcome. The techniques and methods demonstrated in this book are actually natural processes that we all undertake in every day scenarios. By breaking them down and making them explicitly clear, you can apply them easily to your revision, with maximum effect. People overlook the easy solutions, because it seems too obvious to be effective and often favour the more complex solutions as 'they must be the best', whereas the techniques outlined in this book demonstrate the total opposite: an easy to break down system, that can build effective revision notes, one step at a time.

Consequently, you should now feel more confident to conquer even the most information rich texts, breaking the paragraphs down systematically into chunks of valuable, easy to process information. You should also feel that the work you are doing is more effective and efficient, saving you precious time, as well as building a bank of solid revision resources. The best part is, that you have a technique that you can use again and again to retain information and make revision so much easier in the future.

You should now also have a good solid understanding about mental and physical preparation, leading up to an exam and understand how to best prepare your body and mind to analyse and absorb information rich sources and retain key information easily. The key is to produce a realistic and achievable revision timetable and stick to it, not forgetting to timetable breaks and that essential day off.

You have learned the importance of establishing a solid learning environment and exactly what apparatus you will need to optimise performance and create a positive mind-set for your exams. The key is to maintain an organised work environment and avoid clutter and invaders, limiting the amount of equipment available to prepare you for the reality of an exam. Remember a cluttered space is a cluttered mind.

So, I hate to say it, the rest is on you; take on board these ideas and apply them to your revision process. Hopefully you still have a few months to make a serious impact on your revision and you haven't left it until the last minute looking for a 'quick fix'. However, any revision is good revision in the lead up to exams as long as you have a plan and stick to it. Take care and good luck.

Printed in Great Britain
by Amazon